Our Puppy's Baby Book

Capture the special moments!

*Until one has loved a puppy, a part of
one's heart remains unawakened.*

A baby book to document
your puppy's life as it happens!

Puppies are earthly miracles with wagging tails,
little hearts full of love and the pitter-patter of paws.

Our Puppy's Baby Book

A baby book for your puppy to keep heart filled memories and photos of special moments with your puppy.

There is space for snapshots of your puppy! This blank baby book gives puppy lovers a place to chart their puppy's growth.

As your puppy grows into an adult you can create a book full of memories and capture the special moments.

There is a page for your puppy's first birthday, first Christmas, first bath plus birth information. Keep track of your puppy's vaccine records and health.

There is even a page to place your puppy's paw prints!

You can take photos of your puppy discovering his world as he grows into an adult.

Pictures are worth a thousand words, it helps us remember the little moments that bring us such joy in an instant.

Don't miss the special times when your puppy is sleeping, bounding across the yard, his first birthday or favorite things to do!

With this puppy baby book you will be able to keep your favorite memories to enjoy the happy moments for years!

Start creating lasting memories today of your puppy!

Yesterday I was a puppy.

Today I'm a puppy.

Tomorrow I'll probably still be a puppy.

Sigh! There's so little hope for advancement.

My First Day Home

Date I joined my new family: _____

First Photo

_____

_____

_____

My Birthday: _____

Place of Birth: _____

Fur and Markings: _____

My Name: _____

I'm growing. How much did I grow!

Age	Lbs	Oz
6 Weeks		
8 Weeks		
10 Weeks		
3 Months		
4 Months		
6 Months		
8 Months		
10 Months		
1 Year		
2 Years		

Puppy Paw Print

Adult Paw Print

My First Bath

Photo Here

_____

_____

_____

_____

My Favorite Toy

Photo Here

_____

_____

_____

_____

My First Christmas

Photo Here

_____

_____

_____

_____

My First Birthday

Photo Here

_____

_____

_____

_____

Vaccination Records

Age	Shot Date	Distemper	Parvo	Rabies	Deworm
6 weeks					
10 weeks					
14 weeks					
1 Year					
2 Years					
3 Years					
4 Years					
5 Years					
6 Years					
7 Years					
8 Years					
9 Years					
10 Years					
11 Years					
12 Years					

Heartworm Testing:

1 Year___ 2 Year___ 3 Year ___ 4 Year___ 5 Year___

6 Year___ 7 Year___ 8 Year ___ 9 Year___ 10 Year___

Vaccination Notes:

_____

_____

Medical Record Notes:

Medical Treatments:

Neutered	Spayed	Other

Medical Conditions:

Date	Accidents or Injuries

Medical Emergencies:

My Puppy

Don't miss the happy moments!
Start creating lasting memories today!

Photo Here

Memories:

_____

_____

_____

_____

_____

_____

_____

Photo Here

Memories:

_____

_____

_____

_____

_____

_____

Photo Here

Memories:

_____

_____

_____

_____

_____

_____

_____

Photo Here

Memories:

_____

_____

_____

_____

_____

_____

Photo Here

Memories:

Photo Here

Memories:

_____

_____

_____

_____

_____

_____

_____

Photo Here

Memories:

_____

_____

_____

_____

_____

_____

_____

Photo Here

Memories:

_____

_____

_____

_____

_____

_____

_____

Photo Here

Memories:

Photo Here

Memories:

Photo Here

Memories:

Photo Here

Memories:

_____

_____

_____

_____

_____

_____

_____

Photo Here

Memories:
_____

_____

_____

_____

_____

_____

_____

Photo Here

Memories

_____

_____

_____

_____

_____

_____

_____

Photo Here

Memories:

_____

_____

_____

_____

_____

_____

_____

Photo Here

Memories:

Photo Here

Memories:

_____

_____

_____

_____

_____

_____

_____

Photo Here

Memories:

Photo Here

Memories:

Photo Here

Memories:

_____

_____

_____

_____

_____

_____

_____

Photo Here

Memories:

_____

_____

_____

_____

_____

_____

_____

_____

Photo Here

Memories:

Photo Here

Memories:

Photo Here

Memories:

Photo Here

Memories:

_____

_____

_____

_____

_____

_____

_____

Photo Here

Memories:

_____

_____

_____

_____

_____

_____

_____

_____

Photo Here

Memories:
_____

_____

_____

_____

_____

_____

_____

Photo Here

Memories:

_____

_____

_____

_____

_____

_____

_____

Photo Here

Memories:

_____

_____

_____

_____

_____

_____

_____

Photo Here

Memories:

_____

_____

_____

_____

_____

_____

_____

_____

Photo Here

Memories:

Photo Here

Memories:
_____
_____
_____
_____
_____
_____
_____
_____

Photo Here

Memories:
_____

_____

_____

_____

_____

_____

_____

_____

Photo Here

Memories:

Photo Here

Memories:

Photo Here

Memories:

_____

_____

_____

_____

_____

_____

_____

Photo Here

Memories:

_____

_____

_____

_____

_____

_____

_____

Photo Here

Memories:

_____

_____

_____

_____

_____

_____

_____

Photo Here

Memories:

_____

_____

_____

_____

_____

_____

_____

Photo Here

Memories:

_____

_____

_____

_____

_____

_____

_____

Photo Here

Memories:

Photo Here

Memories:
_____

_____

_____

_____

_____

_____

_____

_____

Photo Here

Memories:

_____

_____

_____

_____

_____

_____

_____

Photo Here

Memories:

Photo Here

Memories:

_____

_____

_____

_____

_____

_____

_____

Photo Here

Memories:

_____

_____

_____

_____

_____

_____

_____

_____

Photo Here

Memories:

_____

_____

_____

_____

_____

_____

_____

_____

Photo Here

Memories:

_____

_____

_____

_____

_____

_____

_____

Photo Here

Memories:

_____

_____

_____

_____

_____

_____

_____

_____

Photo Here

Memories:

_____

_____

_____

_____

_____

_____

_____

_____

Photo Here

Memories:

```
┌─────────────────────────────────┐
│                                 │
│                                 │
│                                 │
│          Photo Here             │
│                                 │
│                                 │
│                                 │
└─────────────────────────────────┘
```

Memories:

_____

_____

_____

_____

_____

_____

_____

_____

Photo Here

Memories:

Photo Here

Memories:

_____

_____

_____

_____

_____

_____

_____

Photo Here

Memories:

Photo Here

Memories:

_____

_____

_____

_____

_____

_____

_____

17321597R00046

Made in the USA
Middletown, DE
18 January 2015